Young Heart, Old Soul

Young Heart, Old Soul
M. Tavon

Heart Poems

The Notebook

I hope,
40 years from now
we're looking at old pictures
Of our young love
Smiling at how things
Never changed.

Speeding Hearts

"You two are moving too fast."
They said.
I was confused
I never knew falling in love

Had a time frame
Because we were
Moving at the rate
Our hearts raced
So the pace just felt right

Like the Ocean

You are unpredictable
like the ocean
But I do not fear drowning
in your wave of emotions
When you open up
I hold my breath
And dive in
Allowing my skin to get drenched
In your power,
After my body soaks,
I yearn for more

I'm not the best swimmer
But your waves carry me to shore
Others fear getting consumed by
your massive waves
Not I,
I admire your intensity
I'm allured by your mystery

And I will always
choose to swim
Knowing you would never
let me drown

Honor Student

To the parts of you
That are too complex to understand
I promise to forever remain
A student of your heart
I'll study your love overnight
To retain the intricacies of your
Existence
I refuse to fail you,
Dropping out
Is not an option
In turn,
I hope you remain patient
with me
'For I'm trying my damnedest
To excel'

in the most advance course
of my life,
In the end
It will be worth it
Because your love
Is perfect

Sincerely, your most dedicated
pupil

Untitled Poem

Sometimes we tend to mold our love
interest into an image they can't
portray because that's not who they
are. Sometimes we fantasize over
the idea of love and end up falling
for someone who isn't for us. Often
times we fall in love with
someone's potential while being
blinded to who they really are.
Sometimes we envision an entire
future with this lover before
giving them a chance to show us who
they are in the present reality.
You must learn leading with your
imagination results in a broken
heart 1000% of the time

Sweet Valentine

Cupid's arrow landed
where emptiness dwelled
At first, I thought
"He hit the wrong guy."
For so long
I convinced myself
love didn't belong
in this heart of mine
Until the day
He introduced me
To a shy but brave woman
With a radiant gapped-tooth smile

There's no way she's capable
of causing harm," I said to myself"

Yet, I was hesitant to give her
The little hope my heart had left

Cupid nudged me closer to her
And said 'trust me for once"
I let go of my fears,
and doubts,
Then I reached for her hand
Since that moment
I have yet to let go
Because I refuse to live
without her again

The Thief

Love snuck up on me and stole my heart like a thief at night. The wild thing is, I didn't even call the cops. I knew she was the right one to have my most valued possession. Despite the fact she took it while I wasn't looking.

New Day

Most love stories end in
Sadly ever after's,
Leaving lovers with
The bitter after taste of
heartbreak

But not us.
Every day with you
Feels like we just met
It still feels like our eyes
Connect for the first time,
Every morning,
When we wake up

Each night feels like
The first weekend
We spent together.

Every meal
feels like our first date
Every laugh feels
Like the first joke
We have ever told

Every day with you feels new
'cause your love is timeless

Real Friends

Even when we don't see eye to eye
I will still be by your side
to provide light when life gets
dark

Even when your feet burn
as you tread through hell
I will put you on my back
to give you a rest

no pressure, I know
you would save my life
without blinking twice.

I may not text back fast
Or answer every call
I may seem distant
for the most part
But as a friend you will always
be in my heart
That will never change

The Fault in my Heart

I was so addicted to the
feeling of being wanted
I latched onto
every friendly smile
And fell in love with every hello
When the inevitable goodbyes
Arrived I was left
Feeling lower than dirt
This drug, I loved
Because loneliness was the ghost
I was afraid to sleep next to
So I shared my bed with
Many women
Hoping a one night stand
Would turn into
A happily ever after

This drug slowly drained my heart
And left many scars
it was slowly killing me
And I knew it

Young Heart, Old Soul
M. Tavon

Loving you feels like...

A daydream
That never will end,
Cool soft raindrops
Landing on my skin

A lifelong
summer romance,
Performing perfect steps
At the school dance

An 11:11 wish
come true
A villa,
With the sunset view

Two birds kissing
In the sky,
Stevie Wonder's
'Hotter Than July'

Everything about you and I
feels right
We are why the sun smiles

My Sky

She reminds me of the sky
Abundant and graceful,
and shines in many hues
I look to her as time passes
Knowing she will be with me
through any storm
My heart feels secure
Because her love will be dawned
Upon me for the rest of my days

Young Heart, Old Soul
M. Tavon

Natural Love

My love is a storm
Natural, wild, and intense
'Cause this heart roars thunder

Battles w/ Doubt

On the days when my gut
says I'm not good enough
On the days my knees buckle
When I try to move forward
On the days
The voices in my head
Says I am doing everything wrong
Somehow a smile
From your mouth
Followed by
Words of love from your tongue
And a kiss from your lips
Settles the chaos
That dances inside of me

Asking for a Friend

If I find myself drowning
in a sea of sadness again,
Can I count on you
to bring me
to shore my friend?

Will you be there to resuscitate
life into my lungs
When I cough out water and blood

Will you be there?
Will you still care?
My friend

Or will you allow me
to drown in my misery?

Trackstar

The way you run away
from my love
you must be exhausted

You'll speed unto a dead end
At the rate you're goin
So take a rest, let me in

I know you're tired
After all those laps
You made around my heart

You want me,
I think you're afraid
It's okay
I am too

To settle down is brave
Because most of us are wired
To run away from the love

we dream of

(written in 2017)

Young Heart, Old Soul
M. Tavon

Heartbeat

My heart
Lost its rhythm
until you came
And taught
it how to dance again

Wild Hearts

Wild hearts may roam,
but in the end
they always find home

Blooming Love

Our love is a garden
Where flowers of compassion
Have been watered
by the storms of our pasts
And bloomed under the sun
Together we have created something
fruitful
I vow to never soil our plain
with cheap temptation and lies,
And protect it from parasites,
This garden is paradise
I refuse to lose it,
I refuse to lie it die
I do not see my love
Blooming without you

The River

My emotions are a river
I let them flow
In the direction
They desire to go

Young Heart, Old Soul
M. Tavon

`

Security

Life presents many uncertainties
To a mind clouded by doubt
But your love
Is the one thing
I never worry about

To an Old Flame

You only wanted to remain friends
To keep me at bay
Hoping my love would stay
As you left me astray by day
And pretended to love me at night
You wanted the cake
we baked
So you can eat it
with your other lovers too
The queen of deception
Breaking hearts and soul collecting
Your connection became an infection
So, I had to part ways
For friends we will
could no longer remain

Young Heart, Old Soul
M. Tavon

Sleep Easy

I rest easy knowing
you will be tangled
in my arms
when I wake up

Young Heart, Old Soul
M. Tavon

No more Worries

When I feel like
I've failed at life
I gaze at you
Smile, and say
"I've done one thing right"

Young Heart, Old Soul
M. Tavon

The Loving

making sweet love
as the moonlight shines
through the blinds,
is our favorite pastime

Lean on Me

If you, my friend
Is ever feeling down
Or no longer possess the strength
To move forward
You can lean on my shoulder
And i promise to help get

to where you need to go

But the moment
I have to put you on my back
I must protect my health
By letting you go

I love you and all
But I won't stress my heart
Or crush my spine

To make you feel fine

At some point
You gotta rediscover
your own strength

Drunk Nights

Being in love
Sure as hell beats
Coming home
To an empty bed
After a long drunken night

Of Chasing loose women

Because of You

I'm addicted to you
In the healthiest way
I crave for a dose
Three times a day

Your love makes me feel empowered
Your trust makes me feel secure
Your smile gives me chills
Your stare makes me feel pure

I refuse to shake
What you have done, to me
The feeling is better
Than ecstasy

You are my favorite drug,
I hope to overdose
And remain alive
I never feel alone
I will forever
Keep you close

Young Heart, Old Soul
M. Tavon

Tender Moments

"I hear your heart beating,"
she said.
"Does it sound peaceful?"
I asked
She nodded and drifted off
Into a dream
I smiled,
Little does she know
She's the reason,
She's why my heart
lives without stress

Easy Love

As complex as you are loving you
still feels easy.

Young Heart, Old Soul
M. Tavon

Lil Doormat

Old lovers took advantage
of my misery
By coming and going
as they pleased
Knowing my arms would be
Stretched open the moment
They reappeared

The Race

In retrospect,

The dozens of heartbreaks
And broken promises
Were worth enduring
On this marathon,
in the end
I found myself
In your arms
On the other side
Of the finish line

Growing Pains

One of the greatest lessons I
learned while growing to love
myself was 'accountability.' I was
not always the victim, and the
heartaches I endured
was bittersweet karma coming back
to avenge the women I manipulated.
I also allowed old lovers to treat
my heart like a stepping stone when
I loathed being alone. Over time, I
saw the error in my ways. The
patterns in my failed relationships
and realized, I played a role in
the blame game too.

Being in Love

I guess part of being in love
Is listening to your woman
Rant about her coworkers
And no matter how disinterested
You are
You gotta let her vent
Without interruption
Honestly,

I will take a lifetime
of that over
Listening to my own thoughts
In a dark room

Netflix Dates

Late night binge watching
With my favorite person
beats swallowing cheap booze
In a dim-lit bar with strangers

Without You

Nights felt darker
When I slept alone
I was lost in thought
Because I had nowhere to go
(Without you)
Emptiness is the dark hole,
I refuse to fall deep in again
Even if I did,
You would grab my hand
I'm no longer haunted
By the ghost of loneliness
at night
Sleeping next to you
Provides a peace of mind
Now, when darkness falls
I draw you close like gravity
Using your body as a shield
Protecting my sanity

Young Heart, Old Soul
M. Tavon

The Notebook II

Because of you
I look forward to
Growing old,
'Cause I no longer
fear dying alone

Young Heart, Old Soul
M. Tavon

Don't Break my Heart

Two hearts, mended
For a galaxy of passion
So endless

Our love is a nova
Growing stronger
The longer we go

Our beautiful hearts
Creating sparks in
The dark
Brighter than the stars

I hope we never
implode,

Or
Erode in smoke,

To infinity and forever
Live without you, again
I would never

Young Heart, Old Soul
M. Tavon

Blind Heart

Allowing my heart to
Make decisions in the dark
Often led to the most
devastating disappointments
But in the end it led me to you
I guess being 1 for 20
isn't too bad after all

New life, New Home

Our hearts, filled with joy
Since moving
into our new home
But home already existed

in our hearts
Long before
we moved here

See, trust built the foundation
Which is supported
by communication
Even when we
have a misunderstanding
We remain patient

Your eyes and mine
Have been the windows
To our souls
Baring each other's truth
And protecting us from the cold

And the roof of our love
shielding us from harsh winters
And rainstorms
Comes from our power
Because nothing

Young Heart, Old Soul
M. Tavon

I repeat nothing
Can break us down

So yes,
I'm ecstatic
about calling our new haven, home
As long as you know
we had one all along

Young Heart, Old Soul
M. Tavon

Proceed with Caution

It took a while
to fall in love with you
Because my heart
could not afford another
disappointment

Stubborn Heart

tried not to love you
but my heart was too stubborn
to listen to me

State of Shock

Your smile strikes
like lightening
When it lands
on the surface of my skin
Sending my heart
Into a pleasant state of shock

Young Heart, Old Soul
M. Tavon

Traveling hearts

When I was bold enough to open
my heart to you,
you entered, without fear
traveled where it was too
dark for the naked eye

Power of Words

When you say "I love you."
Even the rage of my darkest
thoughts
Don't stand a chance against
The force of your heart
And the softness of your touch
I feel so empowered

When you say, "I love you."
Fear instantly dies
And becomes the ghost of my past
Because I feel so secure
Every time those words
Leave your tongue
So effortlessly

When you say 'I love you
I smile with the pride
Of a lion
As butterflies dance
Inside the linen of my stomach
it feels good
To be open with someone
Who values every moment
We share

Real Couple Things

That night at the dollar store
When we could not choose between
The grey shower curtain
or the one with black
and white patterns
It hit me
We are a real couple
Picking out the little things
For our new home
This love has grown
So strong in 5 months
From two strangers
On twitter
To acquaintances
In the DMs
To flirting on FaceTime
Then you flew to Florida
For a visit
We made wild love that weekend
Suddenly we became inseparable
Even with the distance between us
We couldn't wait too long
So I moved to Connecticut
To build our life together
For three months
We managed

Young Heart, Old Soul
M. Tavon

To stay sane
In a tiny apartment
That smelled like cigarettes
As we shared the place
With a dysfunctional couple

And we stayed in our tiny room
For most of our hours
Some days were more difficult
Than others but nothing tore us
apart
Now we're in a home of our own
That smells like home cooking
It's funny how life works out
Love comes from mysterious places

Young Heart, Old Soul
M. Tavon

A letter to you,

Because I haven't written about
you, about us, in a while. Maybe
because I'm still soaking it all
in. Every moment with you seems too
surreal to put into words. I often
just sit and smile at the thought
of us being two distant strangers
who blossomed into one union as
fast as the sunsets. My days starts
with you, my nights end with you,
and this is how I want it to be for
the rest of my life. We're still
learning each other, we still
practice patience. Our honeymoon
phase is still going strong. We've
settled into our new home so
effortlessly. I swear we've loved
in another lifetime before that
would be the only explanation of
how everything is coming so easy
for us. I thank you for being the
best woman. My # 1 fan, my
therapist, my lover, my chef, my
comedian, my best friend. I can't
wait to make you a mother and most
of all my wife

The Moon

When I was lonely
It was your comfort
I yearned for
in the moment.

Young Heart, Old Soul
M. Tavon

Send it on

Your love is a letter
with a coded message.
send it to me so I can solve
The mystery.
You have all the reasons in the
world
To be reserved
until I earn
Until I prove,
I deserve your love
keep it all a secret
But let me read it
Don't be stingy
I need it ~~
Your love is a letter
with a coded message
And I'm the one who will
read it well

Heart Melodies

Some nights,
you rest your head on my chest
As my heart carries a melody
For your ears to enjoy

This is Us

I dream of becoming the father
who is his family's
Favorite superhero
A man who gives their children
The freedom to be
who they want to be
The man who shelters
his family from
Deadly storms and fires
The type of dad
Who provides emotional support
With wisdom and laughter
The type of father
Who will build his kids self-esteem
Out of bricks, instead of glass
So, stones of hate
Won't shatter their confidence
A father who supports
Every endeavor,
Any orientation or preference
Every interest
His children choose to do
I dream of being
The type of father who
Holds no bounds
When it comes to loving his family

Seasonal Affective Disorder

For the days
When joy
seem to escape
The reach of your grasp
I will be here
to lend you
some of mine
you will not feel deprived
I hate seeing you in

Such unexplainable disdain,
Mood swings
And tears that seem
To fall,
Without a cause

I feel helpless
'cause I can't save you
From yourself
When sadness
Caves you in
And cuts off your air supply

We can't find the source
to your unhappiness when

Young Heart, Old Soul
M. Tavon

S.A.D comes around

But I vow to never give up
My shoulders are broad enough

to cry on
My chest is strong enough to
support
Your head when it's aching
And my arms will always
wrap around your body

When you feel the need to rest

I have enough joy
For the both of us
So please let me know
When you need some of mine

Young Heart, Old Soul
M. Tavon

To those who love me most,

I may have moved
A thousand miles away
but my love for you
Will forever run deep
Down in the depths of my soul
I hope you know distance
Does not make a difference
Our soul ties are still inseparable
I am proud of the strides

you have made
Since we last saw face to face
And it makes my heart smile
Knowing you've inspired to grow
Mentally and physically
And don't worry about me

 being homesick
Because my heart has settled

into this new home with ease
My mind is a peace

I'm your friend, unconditionally
Distance has no effect on that

Young Heart, Old Soul
M. Tavon

I promise,
If you ever get lost
in the darkness
Again
I will be there to guide
You to the light.

And I know you will always
there for me too

Young Heart, Old Soul
M. Tavon

Soul Poems

Young Heart, Old Soul
M. Tavon

Bliss

Loneliness becomes bliss the moment
you fall in love with yourself

Note to Self

Don't let the voices in your head
destroy you. A strong, beautiful
soul you are. Self-Doubt will not
outweigh your self-worth.

My Roots

People may
Snatch my leaves,
And tear a few branches,
But I assure
No human has the strength
to destroy my roots

No Dead Weight

Elephants are unable
To carry the weight of humans
On their sturdy backs
Without feeling stressed
So why should you?

Writing Helps

A therapist was out my budget
And allowing a stranger
To hear my struggle
Was beyond my comfort
So, I wrote
Late nights

My thoughts and a laptop
Were all needed
To help defeat
The sadness that resided
Inside of me

Tiny Dancer

Life is a stage
And I am the dancer
Recovering from his mistakes
In the most graceful way

Young Heart, Old Soul
M. Tavon

Flying High

I will reach for the sun
As far as my arms can stretch wide
With love and pride by my side
Toxic egos and silent hate
Will not make me cry, again

These wings were made to fly
High in a friendly sky.
I see the light
And I'm not afraid

to soar to it now

Deadweight won't hold me down
I will float lightly over the
clouds

Float
Soar
Ascend... to my dreams

I see clearly now
And I believe wholeheartedly

Dreams Pt. I

The other night
I dreamt of driving a car
I was stuck in reverse
My mother was screaming
At the top of her lungs
On the side of the curb
As the car swerved side to side
The gear shift was broken
And the gas pedal
Was stuck to the floor
Full speed
In reverse

I guess sometimes I feel like

I'm moving backwards
And no matter how hard
I try to push forward
An unexplainable
force pulls
Me back
Everything in my front view
Appears small and insignificant
Most days my future
seem distant
As if I'll never get the chance
To make it there

Young Heart, Old Soul
M. Tavon

That dream symbolized
my greatest fear
It also showed
How I would lose
Everything I love
If I don't appreciate
How far I have come
Instead of dwelling on how far
I still have to go
Because that alone
will Pull me in reverse

Self-Doubt

Self-doubt is like a wasp
Buzzing in your ear
The more you swat it away
The more aggressive it becomes

Young Heart, Old Soul
M. Tavon

Twitter, Twitter

Twitter is one hell of a beast
One minute everyone is
pro mental health awareness
the next they are trying to tear
down
the mental health of another human

How sick is that?
Twitter will make jokes
About someone's
Struggle with mental illness
Until that person
Attempts suicide

The narrative suddenly switches to
"Mental health is important."
"If you need help plz call the
hotline."

People are so inconsistent
there is no wonder
why celebrities
go off the deep end.

Honestly, if I were famous
I'd delete my twitter account
In a heartbeat

Life Lesson

Smile Bright
Life is a light
That only
Shines bright
When you smile
So after the pain
Clear your mind
Leave it all behind
Smile

Young Heart, Old Soul
M. Tavon

Good Hearts

Every good heart
Deserves true love
Sadly, good hearts tend
To attract,
Shitty people,
broken people,
Misleading people,
And
Fleeting people
More often than the good ones
Making it more difficult to
Navigate through life
While trying to find
perfect match

Wild, Happy, Life

What a stroke of luck
it is to be conceived
What a miracle it is

to be born
And what a blessing
it is to survive
Even through it all
Most of us are still ungrateful
Of this rare, rugged, beautiful
gift we have

War Wounds

One of the hardest battles
is believing in yourself
Having the strength
to realize you're good enough
After exhausting your efforts

You wear your heart
on a sleeve
Trying to show the world
why they should love you

Many scars and wounds
are inflicted

Some will be left
opened and unhealed

In the end
You neglect
the only person
who matters most

If you don't believe in you
No one else will

The Phases of

The moon has different moods, too
Some nights it shyly
hides behind the clouds
And some night it's gallant
Enough to take the forefront
Sometimes it shares the stage
With the stars
And sometimes it performs
As a solo act

No matter what phase the moon
Is in
It finds a way
To show the world
Its beautiful imperfections

We, as humans marvel
at the moon's
phases and hues
Round,
Red,
Crescent,
Blue,

Young Heart, Old Soul
M. Tavon

And I ask why can't

We love ourselves
And each other the way

we love the moon?

Chess

Never become a pawn in someone's
miserable life for the sake of
saving them they will drain your
soul, leaving your body listless in
the dust as they prosper off the
energy you loaned them

Young Heart, Old Soul
M. Tavon

Old Stray Lovers

Old lovers
Are like stray dogs
When you finally move on
Sad, thirsty,
and desperate for attention
The only difference,
stray dogs
never screwed me over
Making it easier for me
to give the love they deserve

Dying World

Cities under fire
Impoverished towns in droughts
People living and dying for clout

Our President is a shit show
Elections with 'lost votes'
Our country has become

a running joke

You, my girl
Is the only thing

that makes sense
in this complicated world

Young Heart, Old Soul
M. Tavon

With each word
I found the peace
I was seeking,
The chaos within my soul
Slowly began to subside

- *Writing saved my life*

Cheetah's Speed

I wish I had the ability
to escape
My reality at the rate of a
cheetah's speed
Unfortunately my two feet
can only go so fast
So I'm forced to deal
With my troubles
Inch by inch
And only hope
I don't crack before
I make it to my destination

Young Heart, Old Soul
M. Tavon

No Rehearsal

Life is the movie
I didn't audition for
But was cast in
Without a script
Now I'm forced to adlib

When the cameras roll
My eyes squint in the bright lights
My breath leaves my lungs
As my heart tries to escape my
chest
I'm clueless
So I pretend to know what I'm doing
To keep from looking stupid

The most thrilling
part to this,
There are
no mulligans
Or edits in posts
My bloopers and failed
Stunts will get left on the reel
For the world to witness
The audience gets to see

Young Heart, Old Soul
M. Tavon

The embarrassment on my face
And the bruises on my skin
I may screw up a thousand times
But I'm going to
Play this role
with my truth
that's what I was born
To do

Young Heart, Old Soul
M. Tavon

Sad Drunk Nights

Long nights,
And empty bottles,
You drown your liver
In liquor
To escape the pain
The pain you're afraid
to discuss,
With each sip
A piece of sorrow
Goes into those bottles
Leaving you hallow,
Hoping for someone
Or a sign to alleviate
The angst of being alone

Sad Reality

There's so much ugly
In the world,
Our hearts tend
to doubt
the beautiful souls
we encounter.
How pure hearts
Have been tainted
By this sad reality
We live in

Believe

Never let fear consume you
Never let rejection stop you
Never let pain kill you

The Process

Plant the seeds,
Water the soil
Allow the sun to feed
Them light,
Remain patient
Water and light,

Continue
To feed water in light
But balance is key
You don't want it to dry
Nor do you want it to drown,
Remember, timing is everything

Eventually a few stems
will sprout from the ground
do not get discouraged
if they can't touch the sky

Continue to feed
water and light
Never give up,
It will take a while for

your crops to flourish

And that's the process to success

Young Heart, Old Soul
M. Tavon

Dear earth,

I feel you shaking from the core
Out of fear, I see the texture of
your surface turn pale and dry
I smell the poison on your breath
I hear you cry as your children
watch you die a slow, painful death
You're in anguish
yet very few seem to care
Humans have become consciously numb
Animals are more civilized than we
are
We have tainted your water
The trees you used to protect us
are no longer alive to keep us from
burning on this ball of fire
The damage is done
It's too late to save you,
Honestly, we don't deserve you at
all maybes it's best,
You fade off into the sunset

Conversations with Her

I aspire to be like you."
I said to the moon.
"Amid the darkness
You possess the power
To rise high and provide
The light this cynical world
needs every night."

She laughed, and said,
"you have that same power too,
it's in your smile."

Young Heart, Old Soul
M. Tavon

Dead Leaves

The same way a tree feels
its dead leaves departing
from its limbs.
I feel old friends
Slipping out of my grip
just like the tree
I won't mope
Or lose hope
Over dead pieces
And old feelings
Instead,
I will smile to the sun
Knowing now I have more room
For stronger roots to grow

Mind Poems

Late Night Thoughts

Around this time
When darkness blankets the sky
And the only sounds
I hear are
The fridge running,
bushes ruffled by the wind
and possums
And her snore
My mind travels to places
Sometimes horrid
Other times blissful
I can't control these thoughts
For they control me
And I'm fine with that
I believe,
Each thought

Is beautiful
So I set them free
Death,
World peace,
Becoming a better person,
Serial killers,
Slavery,
Drug addicts,
Sex,
Flying,
Winning the lotto,
The Office,
So on and so forth

Young Heart, Old Soul
M. Tavon

these thoughts
Run free
Unchained and unafraid
I wish I could live with same
freedom
My thoughts d

I wish this feeling wasn't here
I wish these thoughts would
disappear
Heart filled with doubts and fear
Red eyes filled with tears

Young Heart, Old Soul
M. Tavon

Rainstorms

Rainstorms are my peace
When my mind struggles to rest
Music to my chaos

The Universe

When the universe senses that
you're forcing relationships or
endeavors, it will present more
difficult obstacles for not
trusting it.

The Distance

even in small towns
Family and friends
Become
distant
In an instant
They're strangers
Ironically,
In a place where people
Can't seem to escape
They somehow disappear

Far Away

Earth no longer
feels like home,
So please, take me
Far, far, away
To a place
where I can feel safe, again

Young Heart, Old Soul
M. Tavon

Like Bears

I wish I could hibernate
The days away
To escape the stress
The world brings

Flowers

These days,
If you want to receive
the love,
Respect,
And adulation
You deserve
Die,
Die fast
Die young
People become nicer
after you die
Because they're too selfish
To love you when you're alive

Empty Sex

When you have sex
out of loneliness
You feel emptier, within
After they leave
You in the darkness again
Wishing the affair never ends

But sex, when in love
Makes you feel whole
that person embraces
Your body and soul
Until their warmth
lessens the cold

Loneliness will no longer
Have a place to stay
Solitude, you will not
Have to chase
Your peace will be safe
Loving making,
Is gold
When done the right way

Earth Poem

Earth is slowly burning down
And we're drowning in a lake a fire

Surrounded by smoke and ash
Watching precious time pass

We don't deserve
Water and trees
Because of selfishness and greed

The human race, a disgrace
I'm ashamed, living the way

I will be fine
If we all drowned In fire

It's cruel to say

but things might be
Better that way

Young Heart, Old Soul
M. Tavon

Inner-Doubts & Insecurities

Why do I give you
the power to ruin
My best moments?

Your words
Are so deeply rooted
In my brain
That when I attempt
To snatch them away
My muscles strain,
My body aches,
Then I succumb
allowing you to stay

Because of you
I make liars
Of those who believe in me
Wondering if they're using
Kindness to deceive me

Thanks to you,
Dozens of fans
Could applaud and smile
While, I frown
Because of the person

Young Heart, Old Soul
M. Tavon

Who chose to poke fun
From the outside

Why am I like this?
I agree with those
who doubt me
But, ignore the ones

Who are about me
I wish I was more
self-assured than insecure

Life of a Working Artist

I contemplate leaving this job
behind,
Wasting precious hours of my young
life
For a check that takes
two weeks to receive
but vanishes in two days

Why am I here?
I ask the moment I clock in
I dread every awkward conversation
Every entitled costumer
Every petty rule

The backaches
The headaches
The thirty-minute breaks
Aren't work the wage

Father Time seems to move

in slow motion
When here,
As if he's torturing my soul
For pleasure

Young Heart, Old Soul
M. Tavon

Task after task
Customer after customer

I gaze at the clock,
Only 33 minutes flown by
I hide in the restroom

For ten minutes
Then repeat the cycle

I can't wait to the day
Til I'm free
Jobs aren't for me

Young Heart, Old Soul
M. Tavon

<u>Same Words, Different Meaning</u>

Our "I love you's"
were better left said
Miles away
than face to face

Things were sweet
from a distance
Because our definitions
of love were different

Something we tried to deny
A thousand times
Until the day
We said " I love you"
Eye to eye

Written 02/2018

Young Heart, Old Soul
M. Tavon

Growing Old

I loathe growing old
I loathe the day my thick black
hair
turns thin and grey
When my legs
Are too feeble to support
themselves

When my vision constantly
looks like I'm shrouded by smoke
I fear growing so old to the point
My vertebrae is tied in crooks and
knots
To the point my 6 foot frame
Is reduced to sixty three inches

My bright white smile
Perfectly aligned,
will turn into
Crooked bridges,
With missing pieces
Falling out, day by day

Young Heart, Old Soul
M. Tavon

I loathe the day
I look in the mirror
And won't be able to recognize
what I see

I fear the day
My beautiful mind becomes
Filled with scattered memories
From my youth

Sacrifices

Everyone wants success
But very few
are willing to sacrifice
Meaningless bullshit to get to the
next level

People put in more excuses than
effort
"I don't have the time"
Is what most say
While binge watching, bar hopping
And sex chasing

"I don't have the resources"
They say while scrolling
On social media for hours
Indulging in celebrity gossip
Sharing memes
And watching pointless videos

Success requires time
Success requires sacrifice
And success is allergic to excuses

So what are you willing to give up
For your passion?

Young Heart, Old Soul
M. Tavon

Boy Who Cried Wolf

I stand tall for humanity
But that means nothing
When my voice isn't heard

I scream,
I yell,
I shout my message,
Yet the world seems
Mute to my words
It's hurts
Because the blood from my heart
Spills when I speak
Unfortunately,
very few listen to me

I'm like the little
boy who cried wolf
'Cause no one believes
In what I have to say
'The little boy who cried wolf
People won't listen until it's too
late

Young Heart, Old Soul
M. Tavon

unlike the little boy
I've been telling the truth
The entire time

Young Heart, Old Soul
M. Tavon

"The life of a modern black man"

I'm still trying to find my place
Here, on earth.
I'm constantly torn between
Should I be offended,
or
should i even give a fuck?
Some people stare as
if they're trying to figure out my
life
While others attempt to walk
Through me like I'm air
"You're well spoken"
is said as a compliment
From people who probably
Haven't read since high school.

I'm subjected to
Awkward racial jokes by white
coworkers
Strange comments from family
For dating a white woman

We've come along way

Young Heart, Old Soul
M. Tavon

since the Jim Crow Era
But the subtle racism
Of 2018 is just slightly better

                    Young Heart, Old Soul
                         M. Tavon

Dear 2018,

I thank you for the new lessons
I've learned, the knowledge I've
acquired, and leading me to the
love I was longing for. You've
taught me patience pays off. You've
proven that happiness is real.
You've given me peace. Before you
arrived, 2018, my mind was filled
with doubts. I felt trapped and
lost. I constantly felt like I
wasn't enough, from the women I
chased, to constantly having my
account in overdraft; to not
receiving the acclaim I knew my
work deserved. You arrived and
said, "you are enough", because of
you I've realized, I can be myself
- as a man, and an artist". You
were truly special.
Thank you for making my 27th year
the best one yet.

Man in the Mirror

When my reflection stares back at
me
It begs for change
The flaws and mistakes
Are all I see
As I ignore the beauty in me
Why does my reflection
wish for change?
So strange
Is it for my
sanity or vanity?
Is it to escape myself
Or to compete with someone else

Young Heart, Old Soul
M. Tavon

Pseudo

I lied to myself so many times
I was living a double life
To shrug off my anguish
Dishonesty became a second language
Suddenly, My world became
more fiction than reality
Escapism was favorite my
Defense mechanism
And Falling in love with my crushes
, from the start
To see how fast they'd
Break my heart
Became my favorite sport
I did all of this to avoid
The man in the mirror
I was afraid to confront

My demons
I knew I had to change
and it was the furthest thing
From easy

Trapped

Trapped in my mind
Lost in my thoughts
Clarity I try to find
But I'm not worried at all

For the answers I seek
Will come from the heart
Being lost does not make me weak
For I'm trying to make it out the
dark

Young Heart, Old Soul
M. Tavon

Riddles

Most riddles are easy to decode
But for some reason "I love you"
Was a riddle that left me baffled
Many times

Young Heart, Old Soul
M. Tavon

Snowfall

Tonight, snow landed on my palm
For the first time
As I marveled at the sight
Of inches of white
And crystal drops,
Her eyes shined as bright as mine
Electric filled the air
When our smiles met
As we celebrated
A moment
We will never forget

Young Heart, Old Soul
M. Tavon

Winter Mornings

Pretty frigid
Sunday mornings

Warm milk tea
when it's snowing

As we rest in a nest
of our own

Two love birds
Happy at home

Young Heart, Old Soul
M. Tavon

Dear reader, I appreciate you for
taking the time to read this book,
and if you can spare a minute or
two please leave a review on amazon
or goodreads. You may also post
screenshots or pics of my book(s)
to Instagram or Twitter by using
#Michaeltavon or tagging
@Bymichaeltavon thank you for the
support.

Young Heart, Old Soul
M. Tavon

Other Works by Michael Tavon

Poetry

Nirvana: Pieces of Self-Healing
vol. 1
A Day Without Sun
Songs for Each Mood
Nirvana: Pieces of Self-Healing II
Young Heart, Old Soul
Don't Wait Til I Die To Love Me
Dreaming in a Perfect World
The Pisces

Fiction

God is a Woman
Far From Heaven

Books with Moonsoulchild

Self-Talks
Heal, Inspire, Love

Printed in Great Britain
by Amazon